GOBBLE UP MATH

Fun Activities to Complete and Eat

Written by Sue Mogard and Ginny McDonnell

Illustrated by Kelly Kennedy

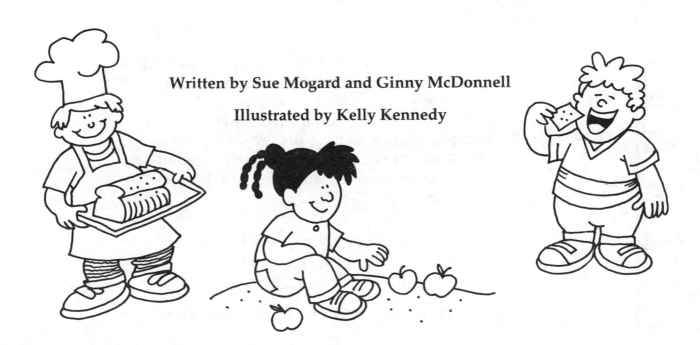

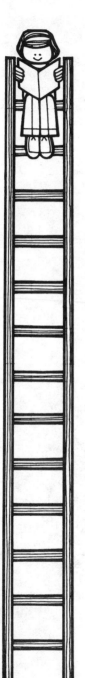

The Learning Works

Cover Design & Illustration:
Kelly Kennedy

Text Design and Editorial Production:
Kimberley A. Clark

The Learning Works, Inc.

P.O. Box 6187

Santa Barbara, California 93160

Copyright © 1994 The Learning Works, Inc.

Library of Congress Catalog Number: 94-075876
ISBN: 0-88160-262-0

Printed in the United States of America. Current Printing (last digit): 10   9   8   7   6   5   4   3

Contents

Contents
(continued)

Contents
(continued)

Mouth-Watering Measurements

Nutritious Number Operations

Contents
(continued)

What is *Gobble Up Math?*

What better way to invite children into the world of math than through a delectable diet of patterns, sets, geometry, measurements, number operations, fractions, and estimations combined with a savory awareness of nutrition?

Children will "gobble up" math concepts and nutritious foods in the classroom or at home as they complete the creative activities found in *Gobble Up Math.* By using foods as catalysts for learning math concepts, children will:

- taste a fraction of a crisp graham cracker,

- feel the smooth circumference of a juicy red apple,

- hear the crunch while munching on a set of same-shaped cereals,

- smell the aroma of freshly popped popcorn while using the kernels to learn division, and

- see the varieties of patterns that can be created using pretzels.

Each hands-on activity uses accessible, healthy, and easy-to-prepare foods. Children can gobble up the goodies after completing each activity or save the foods in containers to use later for more math fun.

It's all here, ready for students to "gobble up." Practicing math skills has never been more delicious. Are you hungry for more? Read on.

A Note to Teachers:
Setting Up a *Gobble Up Math* Center

Thoughtful planning in setting up a functional *Gobble Up Math* center will prove to be a valuable time-saver in the long run. By providing easily accessible supplies, your students will be able to complete many of the activities on their own or with minimal help from you.

It is recommended that you involve your students in setting up a center for *Gobble Up Math* activities. In addition to collecting items such as wax paper and mixing bowls, students can help by bringing in nonperishable foods such as crackers, cereal, and popcorn. Students can organize the center by labeling shelves and storage containers.

The center will be most functional if it is located near a table or counter with a water supply. Reproduce and display the poster on page 11 which encourages students to wash their hands before beginning each activity. Ask the students to brainstorm their own list of rules to promote safety and good hygiene when using the center. Have them design and display a sign listing their rules for the center.

A well-organized and well-stocked *Gobble Up Math* center will provide a fun and exciting place for your students to learn about math concepts in a delicious way.

A Note to Parents:
Using *Gobble Up Math* at Home

The fun-filled and practical activities presented in *Gobble Up Math* can easily be used to teach math concepts in your own kitchen.

Before your child begins a project, go over the instructions and gather the needed materials. Be flexible with food items needed for projects. If your child doesn't like cheese spread, substitute peanut butter or another spread that he or she does like in its place.

After your child has completed a project, follow up the activity by discussing his or her experience by asking questions such as: What did you learn? Were there any surprises? Do you have any ideas for making this activity more fun or delicious? Could you use what you learned to do this activity in another way?

By helping your child "gobble up" math concepts, you will be reinforcing the idea that math is much more than computation and memorization—that math can be enjoyed in many creative and delicious ways!

What Supplies Are Needed?

- plastic or wooden cutting board
- paper plates and cups
- freezer containers
- large and small mixing bowls
- large pot
- balancing scale
- pitcher
- cookie sheet
- wax paper
- paper towels
- small paper bag
- rolling pin
- carrot peeler
- a popcorn popper
- blender
- a juicer (manual or electric)

- a gram measuring scale
- plastic serrated knife
- large serving spoon
- measuring tools for liquids and solids: tablespoon, teaspoon, measuring cups
- miscellaneous kitchen utensils, such as a slotted spoon, a potato masher, etc.
- scissors
- felt-tipped markers
- cardboard
- tacky glue
- masking tape
- ruler
- string
- toothpicks
- clean-up materials: liquid detergent, towels, sponge, etc.

"Gobble up" germs by washing your hands with soap and warm water.

What is the Food Guide Pyramid?

The Food Guide Pyramid was approved in 1992 by the United States Department of Agriculture as the basic guide for maintaining a healthy diet. The pyramid suggests the number of daily servings needed in each of six major food groups.

The foods used in each activity in *Gobble Up Math* have been selected according to the recommendations given in the Food Guide Pyramid. Thus, foods containing fats, oils, and refined sugar have been used sparingly, while foods from the bread, cereal, rice, and pasta group have been emphasized. For foods such as instant pudding and cream cheese, low-fat, fat-free, and sugar-free products can be substituted if you prefer.

You will be familiarizing children with the Food Guide Pyramid throughout *Gobble Up Math* activities. It would be fun to have the children make a large poster of the pyramid to display at home or in the classroom.

Daily servings required in the food pyramid vary according to individual needs at different stages of growth and activity levels.

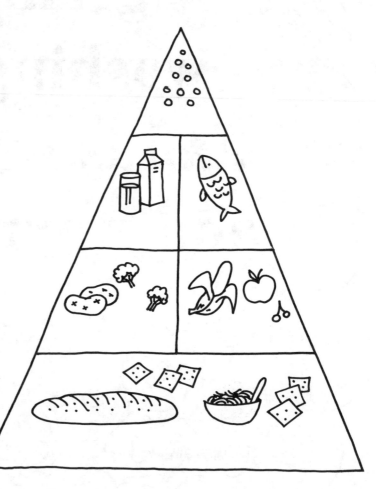

The Food Guide Pyramid:
A Guide to Daily Food Choices

Fats, Oils, and Sweets
Use sparingly

Milk, Yogurt, and Cheese Group
2–3 servings

Meat, Poultry, Fish, Dry Beans, Eggs, and Nuts Group
2–3 Servings

Vegetable Group
3–5 Servings

Fruit Group
2–4 Servings

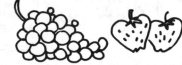

Bread, Cereal, Rice, and Pasta Group
6–11 Servings

Source: U.S. Department of Agriculture/U.S. Department of Health and Human Services

How Much is One Serving?

One serving of the bread, cereal, rice, and pasta group is:

- 1 slice of bread,
- 1 ounce of ready-to-eat cereal,
- 1/2 cup of cooked cereal, rice, or pasta, or
- 3–4 small crackers

One serving of the vegetable group is:

- 1 cup of raw, leafy vegetables,
- 1/2 cup of other vegetables, cooked or raw, or
- 3/4 cup vegetable juice

One serving of the milk, yogurt, and cheese group is:

- 1 cup of milk or yogurt,
- $1^1/_2$ ounces of natural cheese, or
- 2 ounces of processed cheese

One serving of the meat, poultry, fish, dry beans, eggs, and nuts group is:

- 2–3 ounces of cooked lean meat, poultry, or fish,
- 1/2 cup of cooked dry beans,
- 1 egg, or
- 2 tablespoons of peanut butter

One serving of the fruit group is:

- 1 medium apple, banana, or orange,
- 1/2 cup of cooked or canned unsweetened fruit, or
- 3/4 cup of fruit juice

Palatable Patterns

What is a **pattern**?
A **pattern** is a design or arrangement of parts
in a repeated order.

Three different shapes of pasta repeated
in the same order in a row make a pattern.

Two kinds of cereal repeated
in the same order in a row make a pattern.

Pretzel sticks arranged in a
repeated design make a pattern.

What other palatable patterns can you make?

Cracker Craziness

Make a mixture of three kinds of crackers in a large mixing bowl. Scoop up a handful of crackers. Select a cracker and put it on a flat surface. Place a different kind of cracker next to the first one to make a pattern. Repeat the same two-cracker pattern several times.

Next, use three different kinds of crackers to create another pattern. Remember to keep the crackers in the same order each time the pattern is repeated. Draw your three-cracker pattern on a separate piece of paper.

Colorful Cereal

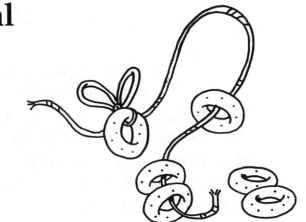

Make a colorful pattern using pieces of O-shaped cereal and string. Tie a cereal ring near the end of a piece of string to serve as a knot. Use the ideas listed below to make colorful patterns with the cereal. Draw and color your patterns on the strings shown below.

Choose your favorite pattern to wear as a necklace and gobble up the others as a snack.

Make a pattern that repeats a color.
example: red, red, blue, red, red, blue (and repeat)

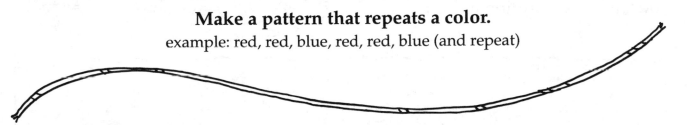

Make a pattern that contains the same color three times in a row.
example: yellow, pink, pink, pink, blue, yellow, pink, pink, pink, blue (and repeat)

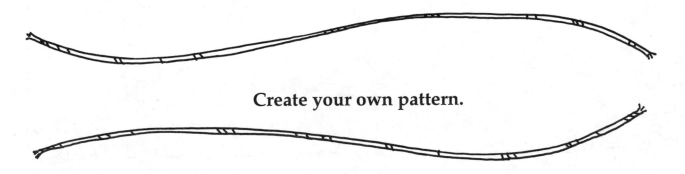

Create your own pattern.

Pudding Patterns

Spread pudding in a thin layer on a sheet of wax paper 12 inches long. Use your finger to draw a pattern of at least three different shapes in the pudding. You might also experiment by making dots, straight lines, or wavy lines. Smooth the pudding out and draw another pattern. In the space below, draw your favorite pudding pattern.

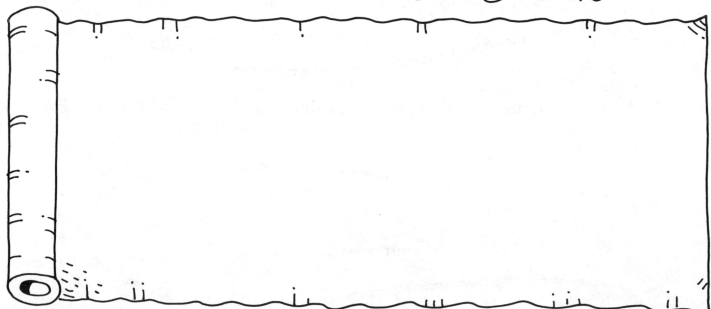

Peanut Butter Repeats

Spread peanut butter on a round cracker. Place raisins in the peanut butter to make one of the patterns shown below. Have fun creating other designs using crackers, peanut butter, and raisins.

Patterns Galore

Use square crackers of two different colors to make the following patterns. Design a fourth pattern of your own.

vertical stripes

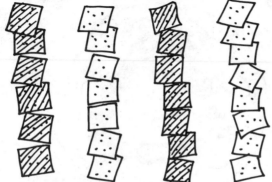

horizontal stripes

checkerboard

my own design

Alphabet Designs

Use the letters in alphabet-shaped cereal to create patterns.

animal word patterns

CAT CAT DOG BIRD CAT CAT

vowel patterns

A OOO II EEE A OOO II EEE

name patterns

PAM BOB TED PAM BOB TED

Create your own pattern.

Pasta Patterns

Select four different types of uncooked pasta. Draw or place the pasta you have selected in the boxes below.

Pasta Key

Pasta 1	Pasta 2	Pasta 3	Pasta 4
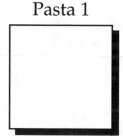	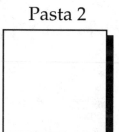		

Place pasta in this order to make interesting pasta patterns.

| 1 | 1 | 2 | 1 | 1 | 2 | Repeat 3 more times |

| 1 | 2 | 4 | 3 | 1 | 2 | 4 | 3 | Repeat 3 more times |

Create a new pattern: ☐ ☐ ☐ ☐ ☐ ☐ ☐ ☐

Have an adult help you cook the pasta, and then gobble it up!

Pinwheel Patterns

Trim the crust from a slice of bread. Place the bread on a sheet of wax paper. Use a rolling pin to flatten the bread. Spread a layer of peanut butter and a layer of jam on your bread. Roll up the bread and cut it into four equal pieces. Lay the pieces on a plate to show the pinwheel patterns you have created.

Sticky Celery Stalks

Use a spoon to spread cream cheese on a stalk of celery. Break several pretzel sticks into small pieces. Place the pretzel sticks and raisins on the cream cheese to create the patterns shown below.

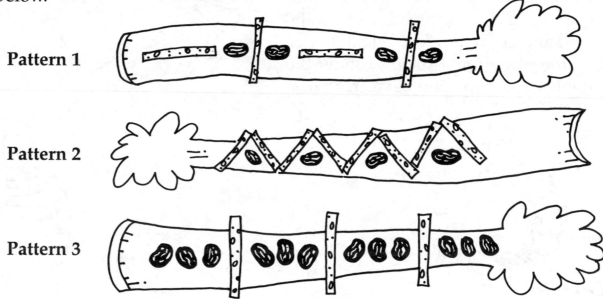

Create your own pretzel and raisin pattern on a stalk of celery. Draw your pattern below.

Pretzel and Cheese Patterns

Use pretzel sticks and cheese cubes to make the patterns
shown below. Fill in each blank with the item that will come
next in each pattern. Then lay out the patterns in rows.

1. 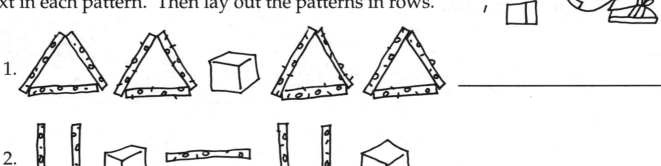 _____

2. 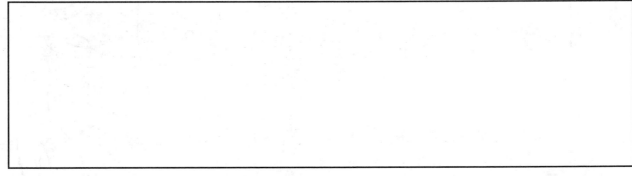 _____

Make your own pretzel and cheese pattern and draw the pattern below.

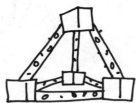

Can you make a three-dimensional
pattern by sticking pretzel sticks
into soft cheese cubes? Try it!

Pattern Plate

Peel, slice, or dice a variety of fruits and arrange them in an attractive pattern on a plate. Draw and color a picture of your fruit pattern on the plate below.

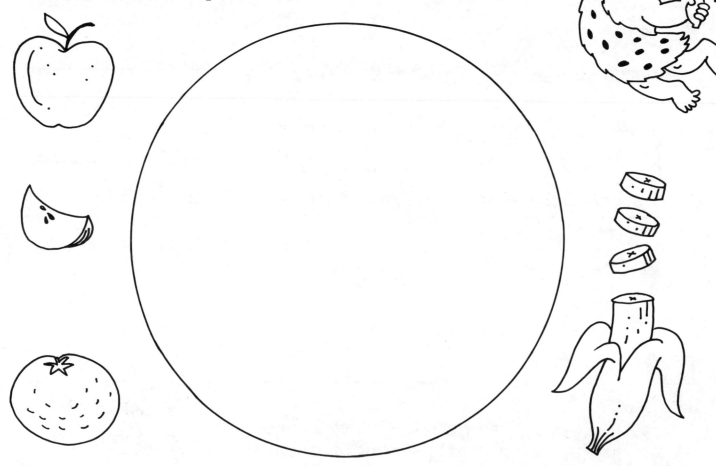

Delicious Designs

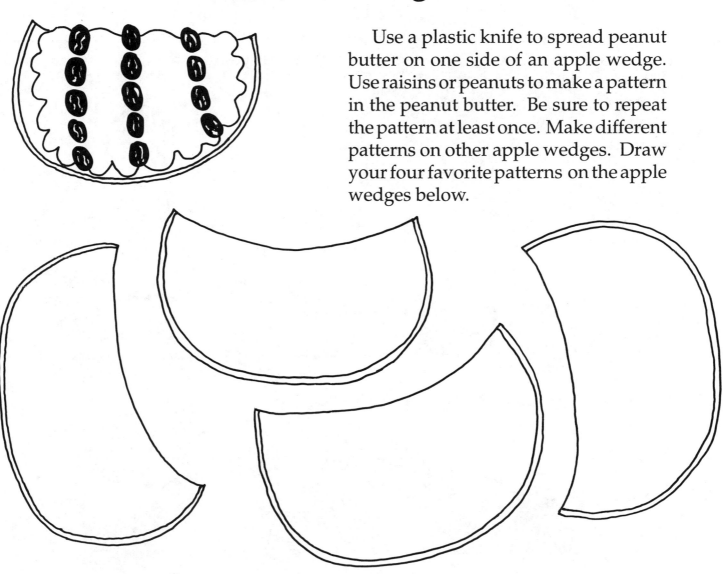

Use a plastic knife to spread peanut butter on one side of an apple wedge. Use raisins or peanuts to make a pattern in the peanut butter. Be sure to repeat the pattern at least once. Make different patterns on other apple wedges. Draw your four favorite patterns on the apple wedges below.

Fruit Fantasia

Use a spoon to spread cream cheese on a graham cracker. Arrange small pieces of dried fruit in a pattern from left to right across the length of the graham cracker. Continue the pattern, going from left to right in rows, until you have filled the entire graham cracker with fruit.

How many times were you able to repeat your pattern?

A Trail of Trail Mix

Create patterns using the variety of foods in trail mix. Draw or place one trail mix item in each box in the trail mix key to use as a guide when creating your patterns. Scoop up a handful of trail mix and lay out a pattern. Use the trail mix key to help you record your first pattern on the line below. Then create and record two more trail mix patterns. Happy trails!

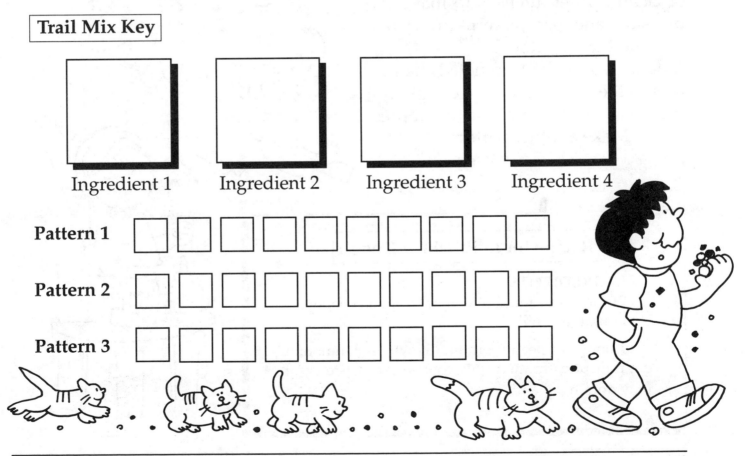

Trail Mix Key

Ingredient 1   Ingredient 2   Ingredient 3   Ingredient 4

Pattern 1

Pattern 2

Pattern 3

Impression Session

Make a batch of edible play dough (see recipe below). Form a one-foot long "log" of dough at least $1\frac{1}{2}$" in diameter. Place it on a sheet of wax paper and flatten slightly. Use a variety of clean kitchen utensils to make impressions and form patterns from left to right on the play dough.

Once you have completed the pattern to the end of the play dough, roll the dough to smooth out the impressions. Make another pattern.

Recipe for Edible Play Dough

INGREDIENTS
$2\frac{1}{4}$ cups peanut butter, 6 tablespoons honey, nonfat dry milk

Add honey to peanut butter. Slowly mix in nonfat dry milk until the mixture becomes the consistency of play dough.

Sandwich Skyscrapers

Use a plastic knife to cut cheese and turkey or ham into small, square slices. Trim the crust from a slice of bread. Cut the bread into squares the same size as the cheese and meat pieces.

Place the meat, cheese, and bread on a toothpick to create a pattern. Create more skyscrapers on other toothpicks. Make bases for your skyscrapers out of cheese. Build a skyscraper city.

Palatable Patterns Certificate

This certifies that

_____

has successfully completed
the Palatable Patterns section of
Gobble Up Math.

_____
Signature of Chef

_____
Date

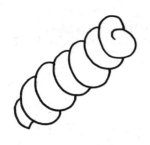   

Scrumptious Sets

What is a **set**? A **set** is a group of objects that are alike in some way.

For example, foods can be divided into sets according to their shape, color, size, thickness, and flavor.

Pieces of cereal that are round make up a set of round cereal.

Crackers that are orange make up a set of orange crackers.

Lemons, limes, and pickles make up a set of sour foods.

Can you think of other ways foods can be grouped into sets?

Food Guide Pyramid Fun

Each of the food groups in the Food Guide Pyramid is considered a set because the foods within each group are alike in some way. Can you fill in the missing vowels in the words below to discover a set of foods found in the Food Guide Pyramid? Use the Clue Box if you need help.

Clue Box

carrots

potato

onion

peas

squash

radish

broccoli

corn

celery

lettuce

1. c ___ r n

2. b r ___ c c ___ l ___

3. s q ___ ___ s h

4. l ___ t t ___ c ___

5. c ___ r r ___ t s

6. p ___ t ___ t ___

7. r ___ d ___ s h

8. c ___ l ___ r ___

9. p ___ ___ s

10. ___ n ___ ___ n

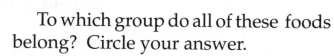

To which group do all of these foods belong? Circle your answer.

a. bread, cereal, rice, and pasta

b. vegetable

c. milk, yogurt, and cheese

d. fruit

e. meat, poultry, fish, dry beans, eggs, and nuts

f. fats, oils, and sweets

Food Guide Pyramid Fun
(continued)

In the first column, make a list of foods that belong to the same food group. In the second column, scramble the letters of each word. Cover the first list with a piece of paper and ask a friend to unscramble your list of scrambled foods.

Foods   **Scrambled Foods**

_____   _____

_____   _____

_____   _____

_____   _____

Ask your friend to circle the group to which all of these foods belong.

a. bread, cereal, rice, and pasta

b. vegetable

c. milk, yogurt, and cheese

d. fruit

e. meat, poultry, fish, dry beans, eggs, and nuts

f. fats, oils, and sweets

Silly Slices

Follow the directions to make sets from slices of bread.

Set 1   Make a set containing four pieces of crust.

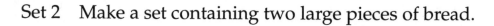

Set 2   Make a set containing two large pieces of bread.

Set 3   Make a set containing three small pieces of bread.

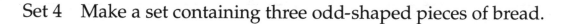

Set 4   Make a set containing three odd-shaped pieces of bread.

Set 5   Make a set of bread pieces shaped like triangles.

What other sets can you make from the bread pieces? Describe the sets below.

_____

_____

_____

Cereal Sets

Combine three or more kinds of cereal in a mixing bowl. Sort the cereal in as many ways as you can according to shape. For example, all the cereal pieces that are round make a set. On the lines to the right, describe the different sets you make.

Next, make sets from cereal pieces that are the same color. Describe your sets. Choose another characteristic such as texture, thickness, or taste, and use it to make a third category of sets. Describe the sets you create that fit into this category.

shape sets _____

_____

_____

_____

color sets _____

_____

_____

_____

_____
characteristic

_____

_____

_____

Choosy Chow Mein

Spread a handful of chow mein noodles on a flat surface. Sort the noodles according to the descriptions listed below. When you are finished, list other ways you could make sets of noodles.

Make a set of chow mein noodles that are almost straight.

Make a set of chow mein noodles that have one angle in each of them.

Make a set of chow mein noodles that are each shaped like an **S**.

Make a set of chow mein noodles that have one curve in each of them.

What other characteristics can you find to make other sets of chow mein noodles?

_____

_____

_____

_____

Plenty of Pasta

Spread a handful of pasta mixture onto a flat surface. Sort the pasta according to the categories listed below. Are you able to make a set for each category? Circle the categories for which you can make a set.

pointed pasta

straight pasta

flat pasta

colored pasta

spiral pasta

bent pasta

thin pasta

thick pasta

hollow pasta

Have an adult help you cook the pasta, and then gobble it up!

Amazing Apples

Cut an apple into at least 12 pieces of any size or shape. Do not throw any part of the apple away. Describe five sets you can make from the apple pieces. Pieces may be used more than once. For example, a seed could be part of a set of apple seeds and part of a set containing pieces that make up the core of the apple.

Set 1 _____

Set 2 _____

Set 3 _____

Set 4 _____

Set 5 _____

Surprising Sections

Peel an orange or grapefruit and separate it into sections. Put the fruit sections in one group. Save the pieces of peel and put them in another group.

Look closely at the fruit sections. Even though the sections may look alike, they can be made into different sets. Can you see ways of making sets? Are some sections smaller than the others? Do some have seeds? On the lines below, describe the sets you make with the fruit sections.

Now look at the fruit peel pieces. Can you make three different sets from the fruit peels? Describe the sets you find on the lines below.

fruit section sets

Set 1 _____

Set 2 _____

Set 3 _____

fruit peel sets

Set 1 _____

Set 2 _____

Set 3 _____

Frozen Food Fun

Pour one cup of frozen vegetables into a small bowl. Close your eyes and pick a frozen vegetable. Open your eyes. Which vegetable did you pick? What other vegetables can you add to this vegetable piece to make a set? Close your eyes and try again. Make another set. How many sets can you make before the vegetables thaw? Keep track of the sets you make and the vegetables that each set contains. Complete the statements below.

When you are finished, ask an adult to help you cook your vegetables and then gobble them up.

The first set contains vegetables that are all _____ .

The second set contains vegetables that are all _____ .

The third set contains vegetables that are all _____ .

The fourth set contains vegetables that are all _____ .

The fifth set contains vegetables that are all _____ .

Salty Sets

Sort a handful of peanuts in the shell into sets. For example, you might make a set of peanuts with cracked shells or a set of small shells. Describe your sets on the lines below.

Then shell the peanuts and make new sets using just the nuts themselves. Describe the sets of shelled peanuts you make on the lines provided.

Peanuts in the Shell

Set 1 _____

Set 2 _____

Set 3 _____

Shelled Peanuts

Set 1 _____

Set 2 _____

Set 3 _____

Cheese, Please

Look at each of the sets of cheese below. For each set of cheese, describe what the pieces have in common on the line provided. Then use cut-up or sliced cheese to make your own cheese set.

_____

_____

_____

Draw and describe the cheese set you made: _____

Tasty Trail Mix

Scoop up a handful of trail mix. How many different sets can you make from your handful? For example, you might make a set containing all of the raisins that were in the handful of trail mix. Or, you might make a set of brown, round, sweet, or chewy foods. Describe the sets you make on the lines below.

Set 1 _____ number of items in the set _____

Set 2 _____ number of items in the set _____

Set 3 _____ number of items in the set _____

Set 4 _____ number of items in the set _____

Set 5 _____ number of items in the set _____

Fruit Scoop

Place a serving of fruit salad on your plate. Use a spoon to sort the fruit salad into sets on your plate. Describe what the pieces in each fruit set have in common.

Set 1 _____

Set 2 _____

Set 3 _____

Which set contains your favorite fruit (or fruits)? _____

Puzzling Pairs

Can you think of something the pairs of foods listed below have in common? It might be their size, shape, color, flavor, or texture. List as many ways as you can that the pairs of food are alike.

puzzling pairs	what they have in common
popped corn kernels and coconut flakes	
apple and orange	
frozen juice bar and ice cream bar	
baked potato and French fries	
lemon and pickle	

Scrumptious Sets Certificate

This certifies that

_____

has successfully completed
the Scrumptious Sets section of
Gobble Up Math.

_____
Signature of Chef

_____
Date

Geometry Goodies

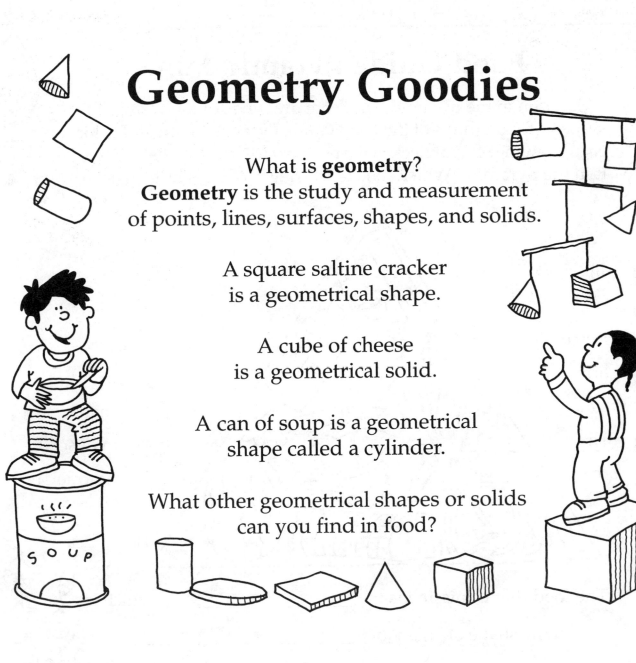

What is **geometry**?
Geometry is the study and measurement
of points, lines, surfaces, shapes, and solids.

A square saltine cracker
is a geometrical shape.

A cube of cheese
is a geometrical solid.

A can of soup is a geometrical
shape called a cylinder.

What other geometrical shapes or solids
can you find in food?

Food Guide Pyramid Fun

Hidden in the pyramid below are drawings of foods from the
six basic food groups of the Food Guide Pyramid. Find and color
each drawing. Put a check in the box next to each food as you find
it in the pyramid. Which food is missing? What is its shape?

☐ milk

☐ cheese

☐ lettuce

☐ corn

☐ steak

☐ fish

☐ bread

☐ pear

☐ cereal

☐ grapes

☐ carrot

☐ banana

☐ can of soup

☐ watermelon

The food that is missing is the _____ which is

in the shape of a/an _____ .

Yummy Shapes

What shapes can you make using pretzel sticks? Try making each of the geometric shapes below using pretzel sticks. Then, color the drawings of the shapes you made.

square   triangle   rectangle

octagon   trapezoid   parallelogram

Create a Creature

Create a creature using pretzel sticks. Gobble up sections of your pretzels if necessary. When you have finished your design, draw a picture of it in the space below.

Here are some ideas to help you get started.

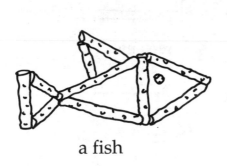

a fish

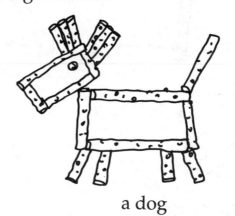

a dog

My design contains

_____ squares

_____ triangles

_____ rectangles

_____ octagons

_____ trapezoids

_____ parallelograms

Dot-to-Dot with Points and Lines

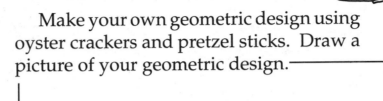

Make the geometric designs below using oyster crackers as points and pretzel sticks as lines. You may need to break the pretzels into smaller sections to complete the outline.

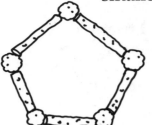

pentagon

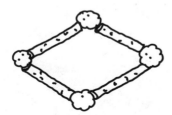

diamond

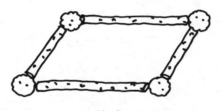

parallelogram

Make your own geometric design using oyster crackers and pretzel sticks. Draw a picture of your geometric design.

What geometric shapes does your design contain?

Geometry in a Bowl

Look at a mixture of cereal in a bowl. Make a check mark beside each shape that you see in the bowl of cereal.

☐ circle   ☐ square   ☐ oval   ☐ triangle

What other shapes do you see? _____

_____

What shape is your favorite cereal? _____

GEOMETRY CEREAL

 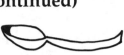 

Geometry in a Bowl
(continued)

Imagine that you have been asked to design a healthy new cereal that kids will love. What three shapes would your cereal contain?

What would you call your cereal?

_____

Graham Goodies

Make a cube using graham crackers and peanut butter.

1. Place a square graham cracker on a flat surface. Spread a thin layer of peanut butter along all four edges.

2. Stand a second graham cracker upright on one edge of the first cracker as shown below.

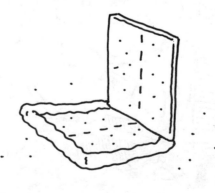

Graham Goodies
(continued)

3. Continue "cementing" graham crackers to the other three sides using peanut butter.

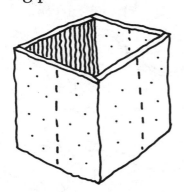

4. Once the four sides are in position, place a final graham cracker on the top of the structure. You have made a geometric shape called a cube.

TA-DAH♪

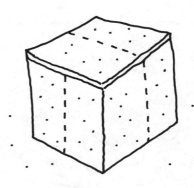

Spaghetti Curves

Place a piece of wax paper on the table. Make some open curves and closed curves using cooked spaghetti. Create a design made up of open and closed curves. Draw a picture of your design in the space below.

open curves

In an open curve, the ends of the line do not touch.

closed curves

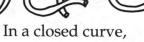

In a closed curve, the ends of the line meet.

Squares Galore

Place nine square crackers in a pattern
with the ends touching as shown below.

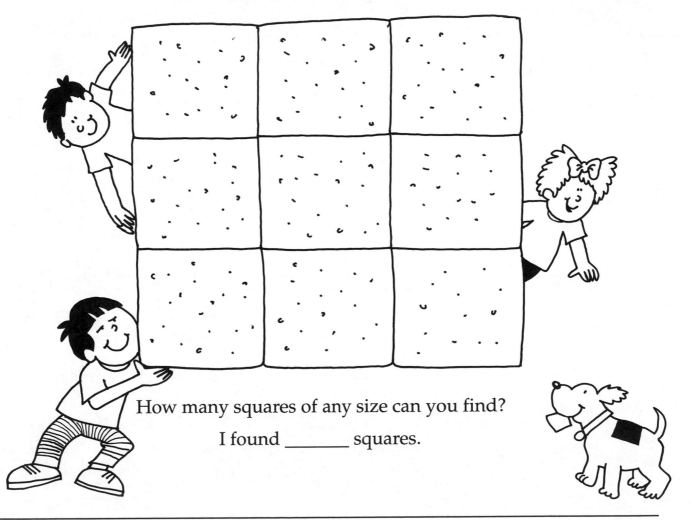

How many squares of any size can you find?

I found _____ squares.

Count Rectangle

Place nine square crackers in a pattern with the ends touching.
Help the Count find all the rectangles. When you are finished,
gobble up the crackers.

I found _____ rectangles.

Crouton Castles

Buildings contain many geometrical shapes.
Using croutons, build a castle.
Use soft cream cheese to help hold
the croutons together
and to make your structure sturdier.

Edible Butterfly

Designs that are mirror images of one another are called **symmetrical** designs. When a butterfly's wings are spread, they create a symmetrical design because the markings on both sides are exactly the same. Each wing is a mirror image of the other. Learn more about symmetrical designs by following the directions to make an edible butterfly.

1. Place a carrot in the center of a plate. The carrot is the body of your butterfly.

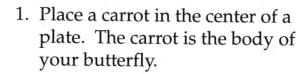

2. Apply cheese spread to a slice of bread. Cut the slice of bread to form two triangles as shown.

Edible Butterfly
(continued)

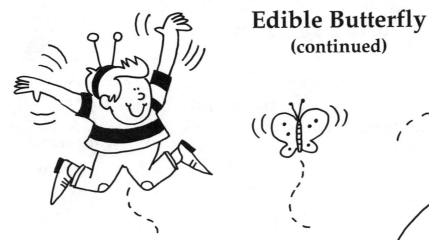

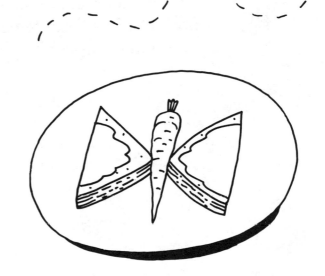

3. Place one triangle on each side of the carrot with the point of the triangle facing the carrot and the cut edge of the bread facing out.

4. Place raisins on each wing so that if the wings were folded together, the raisins would touch.

Frozen Figures

What shapes can you make by freezing fruit juice?
Use freezer containers of various shapes and sizes to
find out. What containers could you use to make the
following shapes?

cube

_____

cone

_____

cylinder

_____

Have an adult help you put your frozen juice
into a blender to whip up a frosty fruit slush.

Play Dough Shapes

Make a batch of edible play dough using the recipe on page 30. Form the following solid figures out of your play dough.

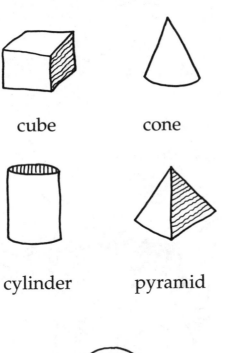

cube   cone

cylinder   pyramid

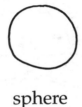

sphere

For fun, make several of each shape and use them to build a creature, a castle, or a crazy clown.

Geometry Goodies Certificate

This certifies that

_____

has successfully completed
the Geometry Goodies section of
Gobble Up Math.

_____
Signature of Chef

_____
Date

Mouth-Watering Measurements

What is a measurement?
A **measurement** is the amount, size, weight,
or volume of something.

The **amount** of bread in a loaf
can be measured by counting the slices.

To determine the **size** of a block of cheese, you can use
a ruler to measure its height, width, and length.

The **weight** of a bag of apples can be
measured by using a scale.

To find the **volume** of a container—for example, how
much milk a glass will hold—you can use a measuring
cup or a measuring spoon.

Food Guide Pyramid Fun

Use the suggested serving sizes from the Food Guide Pyramid to complete the following crossword puzzle.

1. Next time you have your picture taken, smile and say the name of this food. Two to three ounces provide one serving.

2. No bones about it, two to three ounces of this cooked food give you one of the two to three servings you need daily.

3. No matter how you slice it, this food provides the foundation of every sandwich, and just one slice makes a serving.

Food Guide Pyramid Crossword

On a separate piece of grid paper, write the names of four foods from the Food Guide Pyramid. Be sure some words are written horizontally, while others connect vertically by sharing a common letter. Transfer your puzzle shape to another piece of grid paper so that you have a blank crossword puzzle design. Number each box that contains the first letter of a word. Then write clues for your words that use serving size information from the Food Guide Pyramid. Give your puzzle to a friend to solve.

1. _____ .

2. _____ .

3. _____ .

4. _____ .

Measure It!

To practice the different ways of measuring an object, use a square or rectangular-shaped plastic container. You will need a ruler, a measuring cup, and a scale.

1. Measure the **height** (from top to bottom) using a ruler.
   Height: _____ inches

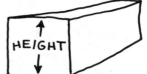

2. Measure the **length** (from end to end) using a ruler.
   Length: _____ inches

3. Measure the **width** (from side to side) using a ruler.

Width: _____ inches

4. Measure the **volume**. First, fill the container with water. Then pour the water into a large measuring cup. How much water does the container hold?
   Volume: _____ cups

5. Measure the **weight** of the container by putting the empty container on the scale. Record this measurement.
   Weight of empty container: _____ ounces
   Now fill the container with water or juice. Weigh the full container.
   Weight of full container: _____ ounces
   To find the weight of the contents, you subtract the weight of the empty container from the weight of the full container.
   Weight of the contents: _____ ounces

Round Rulers

The distance around the outside edge of a circle is called the **circumference**. Use a string to help you measure the circumference of an English muffin. Place the string at one point on the muffin and carefully wrap the string around the edge of the muffin until you reach the beginning point. Use a felt-tipped pen to mark this measurement on the string and cut it at that point with scissors. Now stretch the string along the straight edge of a ruler. The length of the string is equal to the circumference of the muffin.

What other foods could you measure with a string to find their circumference?

Crushed Crackers

Place three graham crackers between two pieces of wax paper and crush them by rolling over them three or four times with a rolling pin. Pour the cracker crumbs into a clear measuring cup. How much is in the cup?   Empty the cracker crumbs into a bowl. Repeat the exercise with six graham crackers.

Three graham cracker equals _____ cup(s) of crushed graham cracker.

Six graham crackers equals _____ cup(s) of crushed graham cracker.

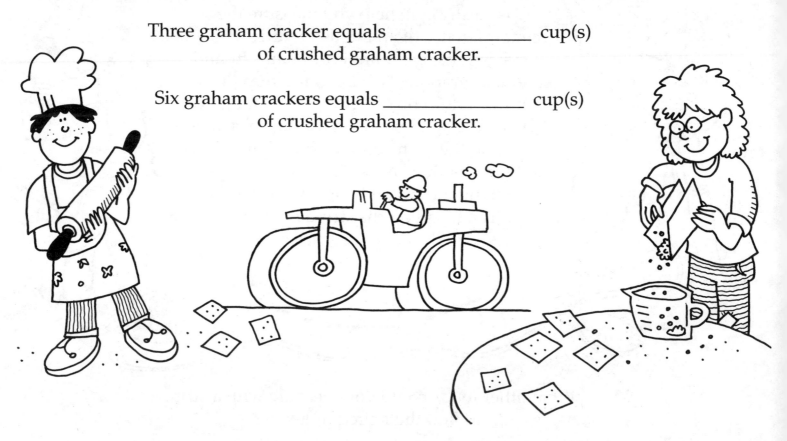

Crushed Crackers
(continued)

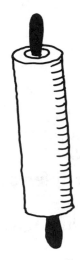

Pour the crumbs from the measuring cup back onto the wax paper. Now crush them again by covering them with wax paper and rolling the rolling pin over them several more times. Return the crumbs to the cup and measure them again. Did the measurement change?

Why do you think the measurement
did or did not change?

_____

_____

_____

Find a dessert recipe that calls for a graham cracker crust and use your crushed graham crackers to make a healthy, low-fat treat!

73

Unpopped vs. Popped

How do popped and unpopped popcorn "measure up" when compared? Ask an adult to help you pop one-third cup of popcorn. Allow the popcorn to cool before measuring it again. Record the results below. If possible, repeat this experiment with a different brand of popcorn. Are your results the same?

One-third cup of unpopped popcorn = _____ cups of popped popcorn.

Did all of the popcorn pop? How do you think
this may have affected your measurements?

_____

_____

_____

Uncooked vs. Cooked

Does pasta get heavier when it is cooked? You can answer this question by comparing the weight of uncooked and cooked pasta. Use a scale to measure two ounces of elbow macaroni. Ask an adult to help you cook and drain the macaroni. Once you have allowed the macaroni to cool completely, weigh the macaroni on the scale again. Record your results.

Two ounces of uncooked macaroni equals _____ ounces of cooked macaroni.

Did the weight of the macaroni change? _____

Why do you think it did or did not change? _____

_____

_____

Try this experiment with another kind of pasta. Describe the results.

_____

_____

_____

Rising Recordings

What changes in size take place when dough becomes a loaf of bread? To find out, thaw a loaf of frozen bread dough according to the directions on the package (or make your own dough using a favorite recipe).

Place the bread dough on a cookie sheet. On the lines below, record the height, width, and length of the bread dough. Allow the dough to rise. Again, record the height, width, and length of the bread dough. Ask an adult to help you bake the bread. Once the bread has cooled completely, record the measurements one more time.

	height	length	width
raw bread dough	_____	_____	_____
risen bread dough	_____	_____	_____
baked loaf of bread	_____	_____	_____

Describe the changes in size that took place in the bread. _____

_____

Gobble up your bread!

Juicy Judgments

How much juice can you squeeze from an orange? From a lemon? Find out by using a juicer or by squeezing the fruit by hand. Use a tablespoon or measuring cup to measure the juice from each fruit.

How much juice was in the orange? _____

How much juice was in the grapefruit? _____

How much juice was in the lemon? _____

What other fruits might have juicy measurements? _____

_____

Squeeze more fruits and use the juice to make a delicious citrus punch.

Balancing Bananas

How many carrots equal the weight
of one banana? How many radishes?
Use a balancing scale to find out. Record
your results below.

The scale is balanced when you place:

a banana on one side and _____ carrots on the other side.

a banana on one side and _____ radishes on the other side.

Using this information, try to guess how many carrots *and* radishes it will take
to balance one banana. You can try two combinations:

I think it will take _____ carrots and _____ radishes to balance the banana.

I think it will take _____ carrots and _____ radishes to balance the banana.

Use the scale to check your guesses.

How close were your guesses?

Balancing Bananas
(continued)

Compare the weights of several different fruits
and vegetables. Record your results below.

The scale is balanced when I place:

_____ _____ on one side and _____ _____ on the other side.
  number   food item   number   food item

_____ _____ on one side and _____ _____ on the other side.
  number   food item   number   food item

_____ _____ on one side and _____ _____ on the other side.
  number   food item   number   food item

Now cut up the foods you have weighed. Can you make
a fruit salad and a vegetable salad of equal weight?

Crazy Carrot Measurements

Choose a carrot. How many carrots tall is your chair? How many carrots long is your desk? Measure different objects using a carrot as your unit of measure.

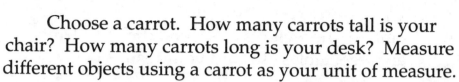

I am about _____ carrots tall.

A table in my room is _____ carrots long.

A window in my room is _____ carrots wide.

A _____ is _____ carrots tall.

A _____ is _____ carrots long.

A _____ is _____ carrots wide.

Now peel your carrot, rinse it in cool water, and gobble it up!

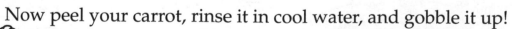

"Eggs-aminations"

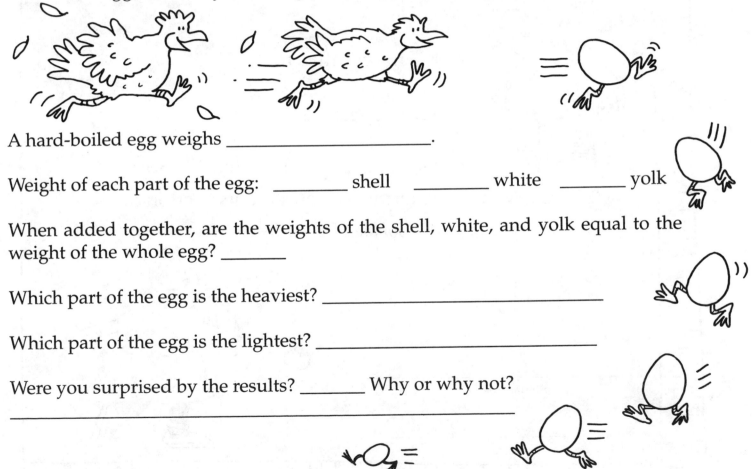

How do eggs "measure up"? Examine an egg to find out.
Weigh a hard-boiled egg and record its weight. Peel the egg
and weigh the eggshells. Separate the white portion of the
egg from the yolk. Weigh each and record the results.

A hard-boiled egg weighs _____.

Weight of each part of the egg: _____ shell _____ white _____ yolk

When added together, are the weights of the shell, white, and yolk equal to the
weight of the whole egg? _____

Which part of the egg is the heaviest? _____

Which part of the egg is the lightest? _____

Were you surprised by the results? _____ Why or why not?

_____

Mouth-Watering Measurements Certificate

This certifies that

_____

has successfully completed
the Mouth-Watering Measurements section of
Gobble Up Math.

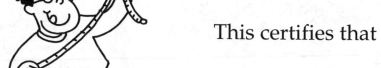

_____
Signature of Chef

_____
Date

Nutritious Number Operations

Addition, subtraction, multiplication, and division are all examples of **number operations**. Each kind of operation has its own "sign." You use the sign in your number sentence to show which kind of operation you're using.

Addition is an operation you can use to find out how many grapes are in two handfuls. The sign for addition is +.

Subtraction is an operation you can use to find out how many grapes are left in a bowl after you gobble some of them up. The sign for subtraction is −.

Multiplication is an operation you can use to find out how many grapes you have if you have four bowls of grapes and each bowl has six grapes in it. The sign for multiplication is x.

Division is an operation you can use to find out how many grapes to put into each bowl if you have 24 grapes and four bowls, and you want to put the same number of grapes into each bowl. The sign for division is ÷.

Food Guide Pyramid Fun

Use the chart below to keep track of everything you eat for one whole day.

Breakfast
Lunch
Dinner
Snacks

Food Guide Pyramid Fun
(continued)

To complete this activity, you will need to use the food chart you filled in on the previous page and the illustration of the Food Guide Pyramid on page 12. Write number sentences to find the total number of servings that you ate in each food group. Example: If you ate two bananas, one orange, and one serving of watermelon, your number sentence will look like this:

I ate 2 + 1 + 1 = 4 servings of fruit.

milk, yogurt, and cheese group: _____

meat, poultry, fish, dried beans, egg group: _____

vegetable group: _____

fruit group: _____

bread, cereal, rice, pasta group: _____

Did you get enough servings in each food group? _____

Cups of Crackers

Follow these steps to make number sentences using crackers and cups.

1. Place two cups on a table.
2. Scoop a small handful of oyster crackers into each cup.
3. In the boxes below, write the number of crackers in each cup.
4. Add the numbers together to find the total number of crackers. To check your answer, count the crackers in both cups.

For each new sentence you make, empty the cups and repeat steps 1 through 4.

Cups of Crackers
(continued)

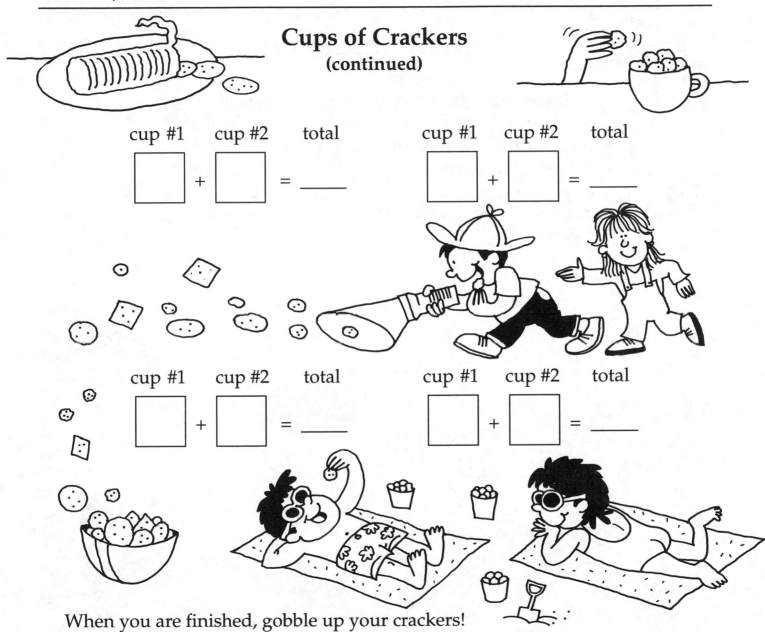

cup #1	cup #2	total		cup #1	cup #2	total
☐	+ ☐	= ____		☐	+ ☐	= ____

cup #1	cup #2	total		cup #1	cup #2	total
☐	+ ☐	= ____		☐	+ ☐	= ____

When you are finished, gobble up your crackers!

Cereal Sentences

Place small handfuls of three different kinds of cereal on a piece of wax paper. Count the number of pieces of each kind of cereal, and record the numbers in the first row of boxes below. Then add the numbers to complete the number sentence. Write down the answer. To check your answer, count all of the cereal pieces.

cereal #1   cereal #2   cereal #3

☐ + ☐ + ☐ = ____

Cereal Sentences
(continued)

Put that cereal aside, and repeat the activity with new handfuls of cereal until you have filled in all of the rows of boxes.

cereal #1   cereal #2   cereal #3

☐ + ☐ + ☐ = ____

cereal #1   cereal #2   cereal #3

☐ + ☐ + ☐ = ____

cereal #1   cereal #2   cereal #3

☐ + ☐ + ☐ = ____

cereal #1   cereal #2   cereal #3

☐ + ☐ + ☐ = ____

Alphabet Addition

Choose nine different letters from a box of alphabet cereal to use in a code. Assign a number from 1 to 9 to each of the letters and fill in the code box below. Place your nine letters in a bag. Take out one letter at a time to complete the alphabet addition sentences on the following page.

Code Box:

1 = _____   2 = _____   3 = _____

4 = _____   5 = _____   6 = _____

7 = _____   8 = _____   9 = _____

Alphabet Addition
(continued)

☐ + ☐ = ___   ☐ + ☐ = ___

☐ + ☐ = ___   ☐ + ☐ = ___

☐ + ☐ = ___   ☐ + ☐ = ___

☐ + ☐ = ___   ☐ + ☐ = ___

Ants-on-a-Log Addition

Spread peanut butter on two long stalks of celery. Place a few raisins on the first piece of celery. Then place raisins on the second stalk of celery. Add the raisins on both stalks. Write an **addition** number sentence to show what you did. Follow the example below.

_7_ raisins + _4_ raisins = _11_ raisins

Remove the raisins, and make up a new number sentence by placing a different number of raisins on each piece of celery. Record your **addition** number sentences below.

_____ raisins + _____ raisins = _____ raisins

_____ raisins + _____ raisins = _____ raisins

_____ raisins + _____ raisins = _____ raisins

_____ raisins + _____ raisins = _____ raisins

Gobble up your ants on a log.

Eggs Away!

Start with a full carton of hard-boiled eggs. Take out two eggs. Write a **subtraction** number sentence on the lines below to show what you did.

_____ − _____ = _____

Put all the eggs back into the carton. Take out four eggs. Write a number sentence to show what you did, and do the arithmetic to find out how many eggs are left in the carton.

_____ − _____ = _____

Check your answer by counting the eggs left in the carton.

Put all of the eggs back into the carton. Gobble up one of the eggs. Write a number sentence to show what you did and how many eggs are left.

_____ − _____ = _____

Nutty Number Sentences

Place 20 peanuts in a paper bag. Reach in and take out a handful of peanuts. Count them. Subtract the number of peanuts you took out of the bag from 20 to find out how many peanuts are left in the bag. Record your answers by filling in the subtraction number sentence below.

_____ − _____ = _____

Place 15 peanuts in a paper bag. Reach in and take out a handful of peanuts. Count them. Subtract that number from 15. Fill in the subtraction number sentence below to show how many peanuts are left in the bag.

_____ − _____ = _____

Nutty Number Sentences
(continued)

Count a handful of peanuts and place them in a bag. Take out some to make a subtraction sentence. Repeat, recording each problem and answer below.

_____ – _____ = _____

_____ – _____ = _____

_____ – _____ = _____

_____ – _____ = _____

Now gobble up your peanuts!

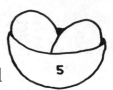
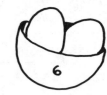

Bowls of Eggs

Place six small bowls on the table. Put two hard-boiled eggs into each bowl. Write a number sentence using **addition** to find out how many eggs you have in the bowls:

_____

Check your answer by counting all of the eggs.

Now write a number sentence using **multiplication** to find out how many eggs you have all together. Remember: The sign for multiplication is **x**.

_____ bowls **x** _____ eggs in each bowl = _____ eggs total

Check your answer by counting all of the eggs.

Did you find it easier to use **addition** or **multiplication** to answer this number question? _____

Why?_____

_____

Bowls of Eggs
(continued)

Put all of the eggs back into the carton. Put three of the bowls away so that you have three bowls left. Put two eggs into each bowl. Write a number sentence that uses **addition** to find out how many eggs you have in the three bowls:

_____

Check your answer by counting the eggs. Now write a number sentence using **multiplication** to find out how many eggs you have in the three bowls:

_____ x _____ = _____

Check your answer by counting the eggs. Put one more egg into each bowl. Write a number sentence using **addition** to find out how many eggs you have in the three bowls:

_____

Check your answer by counting the eggs. Now write a number sentence using **multiplication** to find out how many eggs you have in the three bowls:

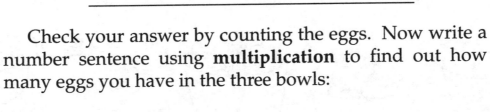

_____ x _____ = _____

Check your answer by counting the eggs.

Dividing Popcorn

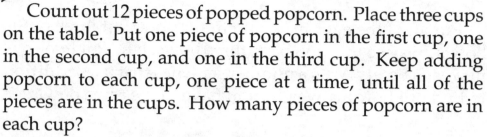

Count out 12 pieces of popped popcorn. Place three cups on the table. Put one piece of popcorn in the first cup, one in the second cup, and one in the third cup. Keep adding popcorn to each cup, one piece at a time, until all of the pieces are in the cups. How many pieces of popcorn are in each cup?

Complete the following **division** number sentence to show what you did. The sign for division is ÷.

12 pieces ÷ _____ cups = _____ pieces in each cup

Empty all the cups onto the table. Take away one of the cups so that you have two cups left. Put popcorn into each cup, one piece at a time, like you did the first time. Write a number sentence using **division** to show what you did:

12 pieces ÷ _____ cups = _____ pieces in each cup

Dividing Popcorn
(continued)

Empty the cups onto the table again. Put two more cups on the table so that you have four cups. Put popcorn into the cups, one piece at a time until all of the pieces are in cups. Write a division number sentence to show what you did:

12 pieces ÷ _____ cups = _____ pieces in each cup

Put a total of 20 popcorn pieces on the table. Divide them evenly among the four cups. Complete this number sentence to show what you did:

20 pieces ÷ _____ cups = _____ pieces in each cup

Empty the cups onto the table. Take away two of the cups. Divide the pieces between the two cups you have left. Write a number sentence to show what you did.

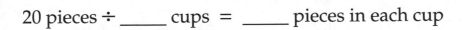

_____ ÷ _____ = _____

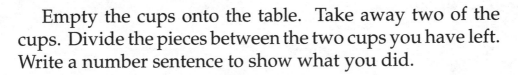

Gobble up the popcorn!

Nutritious Number Operations Certificate

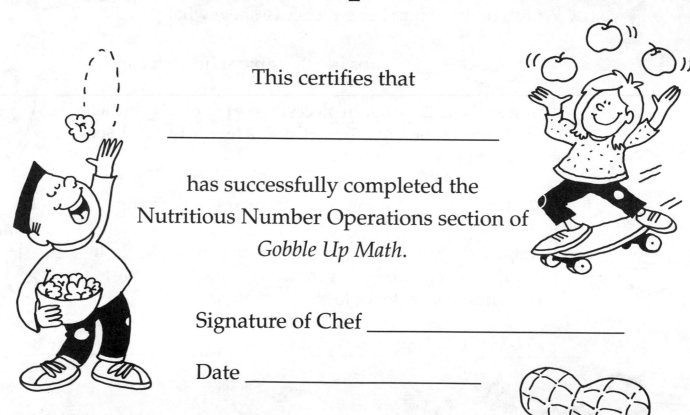

This certifies that

_____

has successfully completed the
Nutritious Number Operations section of
Gobble Up Math.

Signature of Chef _____

Date _____

Flavorful Fractions

What is a **fraction**?
A **fraction** represents a portion of a whole.

If a graham cracker is divided into
four equal parts, each part is called one-fourth.

If an apple is divided into two equal parts,
each part is called one-half.

What other flavorful fractions can you discover?

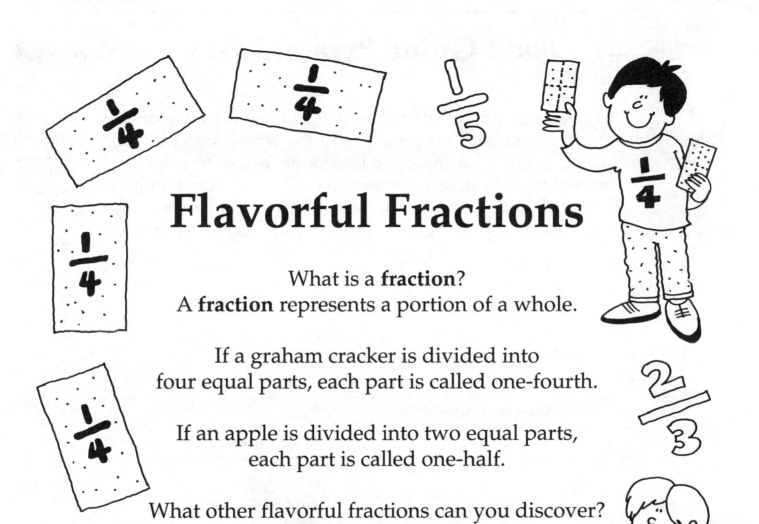

Food Guide Pyramid Fun

To complete this activity you will need the illustration of the Food Guide Pyramid on page 12 and the wheel found on the following page. Use the color key found below to color the sections of the wheel. Color a section for each serving required daily in each food group. The completed circle will show comparisons among the daily serving requirements in each food group.

Color Key

red	bread, cereal, rice, and pasta	(7 servings daily)
orange	vegetable	(4 servings daily)
yellow	fruit	(3 servings daily)
green	milk, yogurt, and cheese	(3 servings daily)
blue	meat, poultry, fish, dry beans, eggs, and nuts	(3 servings daily)

Food Guide Pyramid Fun
(continued)

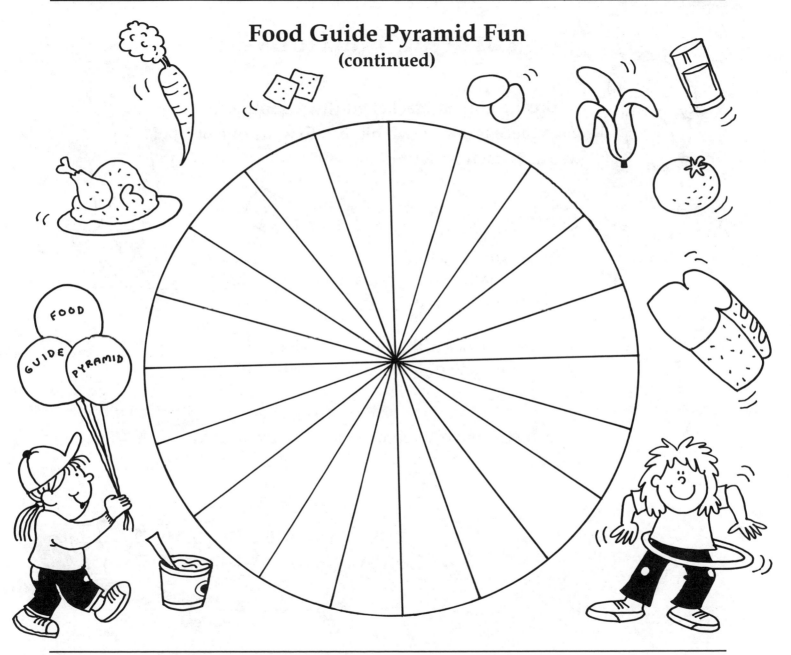

Forming Fractions

Break a graham cracker into two equal pieces. Each piece is one of two pieces. To write one of two as a fraction, write $\frac{1}{2}$.

Now, break each of your two graham cracker pieces in half. How many pieces of graham cracker do you have? _____

Gobble up one of the pieces of graham cracker. You just ate one of four pieces. Write that as a fraction. _____

You still have three of the four pieces left. Write that as a fraction. _____

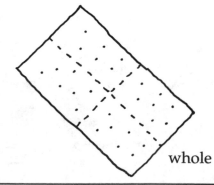

whole

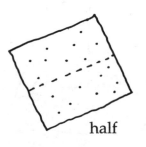

half

quarters

Dice the Slices

Lay three slices of cheese in a row. Leave the first slice in one piece. Cut the second slice into two equal pieces. Cut the third slice into four equal pieces.

The slice that's cut into two pieces is cut in half. One of two equal pieces is one-half. Write the fraction for one-half. _____

The slice that's cut into four pieces is cut into fourths. How many fourths make a whole slice? _____

Now gobble up two of the fourths. Write a fraction showing how many fourths of the cheese slice are left. _____

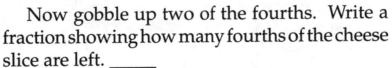

Sweet Sections

Look at a whole graham cracker. How many sections does the graham cracker have? Are the sections the same size? To compare the size of each section, carefully break the graham cracker along the lines. Place the pieces on top of one another. Are they the same size? If the pieces are the same size, each piece is an equal fraction of the whole graham cracker. For example, if you have four sections, the graham cracker is divided into fourths.

Place the graham cracker sections together again to make one whole graham cracker. Take away two of the four sections of the graham cracker. Write a subtraction number sentence to show what you did.

$$\frac{}{4} - \frac{}{4} = \frac{}{4}$$

Sweet Sections
(continued)

Place the graham cracker fourths together again to make one whole. Take away one of the four pieces (1/4) of the graham cracker. Write a number sentence to show what you did.

$$\frac{}{4} - \frac{}{4} = \frac{}{4}$$

Place the graham cracker fourths together again to make one whole. Take away three of the four pieces (3/4) of the graham cracker. Write a number sentence to show what you did.

$$\frac{}{4} - \frac{}{4} = \frac{}{4}$$

Gobble up the graham crackers!

Orange Parts

Cut two oranges in half. Put the orange halves into a bowl. Take out two halves. Put the halves together to form a whole orange. Two half oranges = one whole orange.

Put all the pieces back in the bowl. Take out all four halves. Put the halves together to form whole oranges.

four half oranges = _____ whole oranges

Fractions in a Cup

Fill a one-fourth measuring cup with milk. Pour the milk into a one-half measuring cup. How much of the one-half cup measure does the milk fill? _____

Fill a one-third measuring cup with milk. Pour the milk into a one-cup measuring cup. How many more one-third cup measures of milk will it take to fill the one-cup measure? _____ Check if you were right by counting how many times you have to pour one-third cup of milk into the one-cup measure until it is full.

Apple Fraction Action

Cut an apple in half.
How many pieces of apple do you have? _____

Cut each apple piece in half again.
How many apple pieces do you have? _____

Cut each apple piece in half again.
How many apple pieces do you have? _____

One whole apple equals _____ pieces.

Another way of writing this is $1 = \dfrac{8}{8}$

Use your eight apple pieces to solve the following addition and subtraction problems.

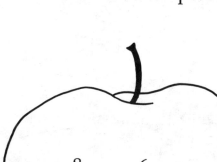

$$\frac{5}{8} + \frac{3}{8} = \frac{}{8}$$

$$\frac{8}{8} - \frac{6}{8} = \frac{}{8}$$

$$\frac{7}{8} - \frac{5}{8} = \frac{}{8}$$

Apple Fraction Action
(continued)

Use the pieces of your apple to complete the following fraction sentences.

3 pieces + _____ pieces = 1 whole apple

$$\frac{3}{8} + \frac{}{8} = \frac{8}{8}$$

2 pieces + _____ pieces = 1 whole apple

$$\frac{2}{8} + \frac{}{8} = \frac{8}{8}$$

4 pieces + _____ pieces = 1 whole apple

$$\frac{4}{8} + \frac{}{8} = \frac{8}{8}$$

1 piece + _____ pieces = 1 whole apple

$$\frac{1}{8} + \frac{}{8} = \frac{8}{8}$$

Gobble up your apple pieces!

Crispy Cereal Fractions

Measure one cup of crisp rice cereal into a bowl. Use a one-half measuring cup to remove the cereal from the bowl.

How many times did you fill the one-half measuring cup to remove all the cereal from the bowl? _____

How many $\dfrac{1}{2}$'s are in 1? _____

Measure one cup of cereal into a bowl. Use a one-fourth measuring cup to remove the cereal from the bowl.

How many times did you use the one-fourth measuring cup to remove all the cereal from the bowl? _____

How many $\dfrac{1}{4}$'s are in 1? _____

Measure one-half cup of cereal into a bowl. Use a one-fourth measuring cup to remove the cereal from the bowl.

How many times did you fill the one-fourth measuring cup to remove all the cereal from the bowl? _____

How many $\dfrac{1}{4}$'s are in $\dfrac{1}{2}$? _____

Gobble up your cereal!

Counting Crackers

Use 10 crackers to make a design. Then fill in both blanks in each number sentence below.

How many crackers are square?

_____ out of ten (or $\dfrac{}{10}$)

How many crackers are round?

_____ out of ten (or $\dfrac{}{10}$)

How many crackers are oval?

_____ out of ten (or $\dfrac{}{10}$)

Use 15 crackers to make another design. Then fill in both blanks in each number sentence below.

How many crackers are square?

_____ out of fifteen (or $\dfrac{}{15}$)

How many crackers are round?

_____ out of fifteen (or $\dfrac{}{15}$)

How many crackers are oval?

_____ out of fifteen (or $\dfrac{}{15}$)

Fraction Fun

Cut a slice of cheese into eight equal pieces as shown. Use the cheese to help you solve the following problems.

Which is more: $\dfrac{3}{8}$ or $\dfrac{5}{8}$? _____

Which is more: $\dfrac{1}{8}$ or $\dfrac{4}{8}$? _____

Which is more: $\dfrac{6}{8}$ or $\dfrac{2}{8}$? _____

Is one whole slice of cheese equal to $\dfrac{6}{8}$, $\dfrac{7}{8}$, or $\dfrac{8}{8}$?

How many pieces equal $\dfrac{1}{2}$ of the slice? _____

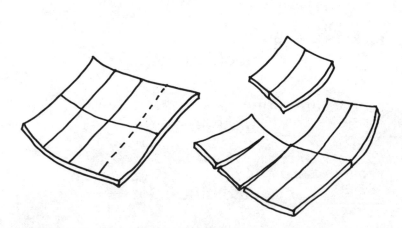

Fraction Fun
(continued)

Cut a slice of cheese into six equal pieces. Use the cheese to help you solve the following problems.

Which is more: $\dfrac{2}{6}$ or $\dfrac{4}{6}$? _____

Which is more: $\dfrac{3}{6}$ or $\dfrac{4}{6}$? _____

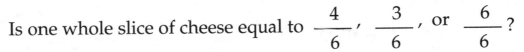

Is one whole slice of cheese equal to $\dfrac{4}{6}$, $\dfrac{3}{6}$, or $\dfrac{6}{6}$?

How many pieces equal $\dfrac{1}{2}$ of the slice? _____

Have fun making up your own cheese fractions. Then gobble up the cheese!

Cracker Fractions

Start with 16 square crackers to solve these problems.

Take away half of the crackers (1 out of every 2 crackers).

How many did you take away? _____
$$\frac{1}{2} = \frac{}{16}$$

Take away one-fourth of the crackers (1 out of every 4 crackers).

How many did you take away? _____
$$\frac{1}{4} = \frac{}{16}$$

Cracker Fractions
(continued)

Take away three-fourths of the crackers (3 out of every 4 crackers).

How many did you take away? _____

$$\frac{1}{2} = \frac{}{16}$$

Take away one-eighth of the crackers (1 out of every 8 crackers).

How many did you take away? _____

$$\frac{1}{2} = \frac{}{16}$$

Gobble up the crackers!

Flavorful Fractions Certificate

This certifies that

_____

has successfully completed the Flavorful Fractions

section of

Gobble Up Math.

Signature of Chef _____

Date _____

Edible Estimates

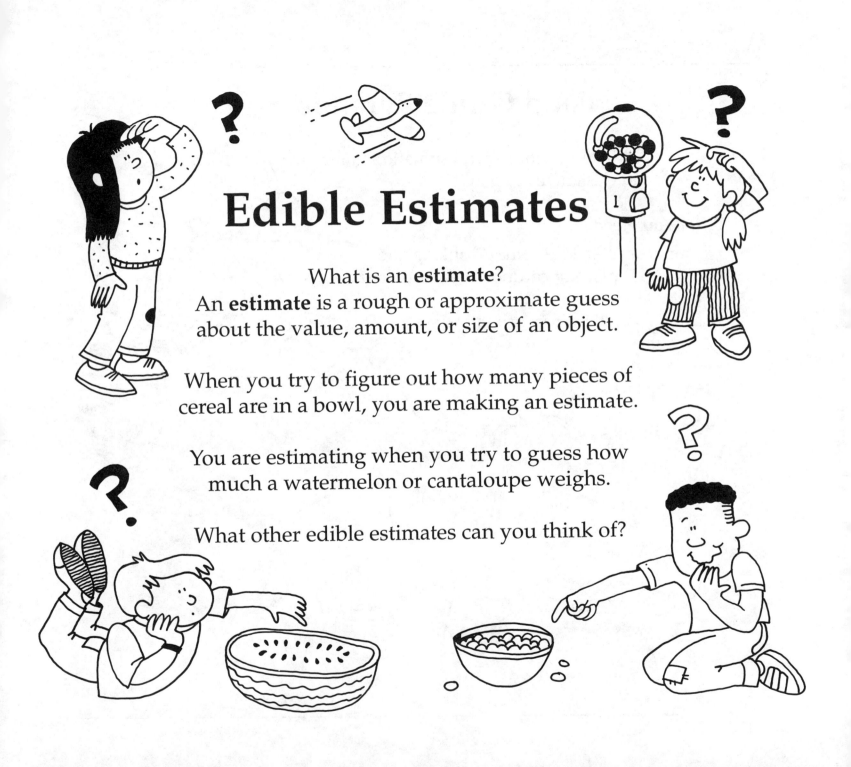

What is an **estimate**?
An **estimate** is a rough or approximate guess about the value, amount, or size of an object.

When you try to figure out how many pieces of cereal are in a bowl, you are making an estimate.

You are estimating when you try to guess how much a watermelon or cantaloupe weighs.

What other edible estimates can you think of?

Food Guide Pyramid Fun

Make up your own estimation games for your friends and classmates to play.

What You Need

- four clear plastic, 9-ounce drinking cups
- $8\frac{1}{2}$" x 11" piece of cardboard cut into fourths
- tacky glue
- small food items for estimating such as:
  - nuts
  - cereal
  - popcorn
  - rice
  - split peas

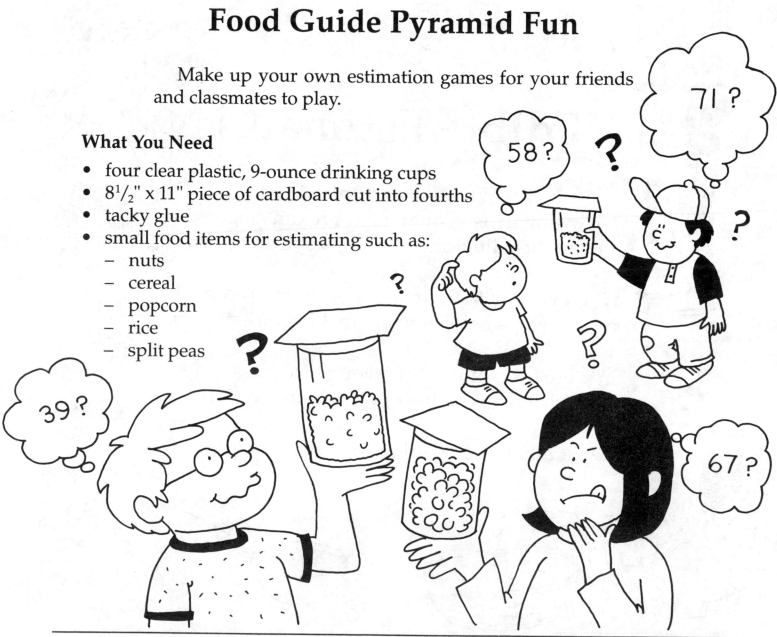

Food Guide Pyramid Fun
(Continued)

What You Do

1. Pick any four items from the list on page 120, or come up with your own ideas for objects to use.

2. Before putting your first items into a cup, count each item. Write the number down on a piece of paper.

3. Pour the first item into one of the plastic cups.

4. Put a thick layer of glue around the rim of the plastic cup.

5. Place the piece of cardboard on top of the cup as shown.

6. Apply mild pressure on the cardboard until the glue dries.

7. Turn the cup upside down so that the cardboard is on the bottom.

8. Repeat these same steps with the three remaining items, one object per cup.

9. Your friends will have fun estimating the number of objects in each of the four cups. Only you will know the actual number of objects in each cup.

Pretzel Stick Tricks

Use a pretzel stick as a measuring stick. Estimate the measurement of the following objects. Check your estimates by using a pretzel stick to measure each object.

height of a bottle:

estimate: _____ pretzels   actual measurement: _____ pretzels

length of your arm:

estimate: _____ pretzels   actual measurement : _____ pretzels

length of a ruler:

estimate: _____ pretzels   actual measurement: _____ pretzels

length of a book:

estimate: _____ pretzels   actual measurement : _____ pretzels

Tower Power

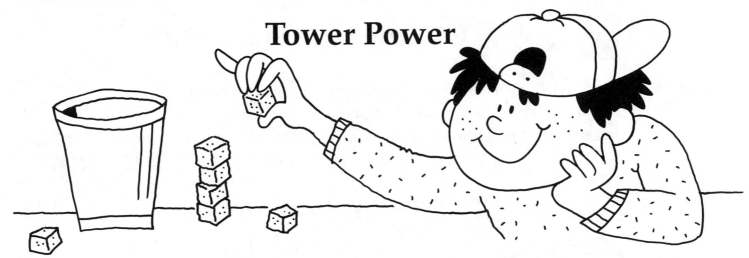

Use a crouton as your unit of measurement. Estimate the
height of the following objects. To check your estimates,
count how many croutons you can stack next to each item.

height of a paper cup:
    estimate: _____ croutons   actual measurement: _____ croutons

height of a chalkboard eraser:
    estimate: _____ croutons   actual measurement: _____ croutons

height of a bottle of glue:
    estimate: _____ croutons   actual measurement : _____ croutons

height of a _____ :
    estimate: _____ croutons   actual measurement: _____ croutons

Goodies Guess

Fill three containers of different sizes with popped popcorn. Estimate the number of popcorn pieces in each container. Check your answers by counting each piece. (Hint: For easy counting, group the kernels in sets of 5's or 10's.)

I estimate that there are _____ pieces

I estimate that there are _____ pieces

I estimate that there are _____ pieces

actual number: _____

actual number: _____

actual number: _____

Color the drawing of the container with the most accurate estimation.

Gobble up your popcorn!

Cereal Surprises

Fill three bowls of different sizes with rice cereal. Estimate how many tablespoons of cereal are in each bowl. Then check your answers by actually measuring the cereal with a tablespoon:

I estimate that there are _____ tablespoons

actual number: _____

I estimate that there are _____ tablespoons

actual number: _____

I estimate that there are _____ tablespoons

actual number: _____

Gobble up the cereal!

Cracker Contest

Fill a large glass jar with oyster crackers, counting them as you put them in. Write down the number of crackers that are in the jar. Put a lid on your jar. Bring the jar to class, and ask your classmates to estimate how many crackers are in the jar. Have them write their estimates on tickets like the one shown below. Make up an award to give to the student whose guess is closest to the number of oyster crackers in the jar.

Name

My estimate: _____

Pasta Pieces

Fill two containers with uncooked pasta. Put small elbow macaroni in one container and large elbow macaroni in the other. Estimate the number of pieces of pasta in each container. Then check your estimates by counting the pieces of pasta in each container.

small macaroni:

estimate: _____ pieces   actual number: _____ pieces

large macaroni:

estimate: _____ pieces   actual number: _____ pieces

Which macaroni was more difficult to estimate? _____

_____

Why do you think this was so? _____

_____

With the help of an adult, cook your pasta, add your favorite sauce, and gobble it up!

Banana Calculations

Use the length of an unpeeled banana to estimate the following measurements. Then measure each item with the banana and record your results.

I estimate that my arm is ____ bananas long.
My arm is actually ____ bananas long.

I estimate that the length of my leg is ____ bananas long.
My leg is actually ____ bananas long.

I estimate that I am ____ bananas tall.
I am actually ____ bananas tall.

I estimate that one wall in my bedroom (or classroom) is ____ bananas long.
The wall is actually ____ bananas long.

Now peel your banana, and gobble it up!

Have fun estimating the lengths, heights, and widths of other objects at home and at school.

The Raisin Robot

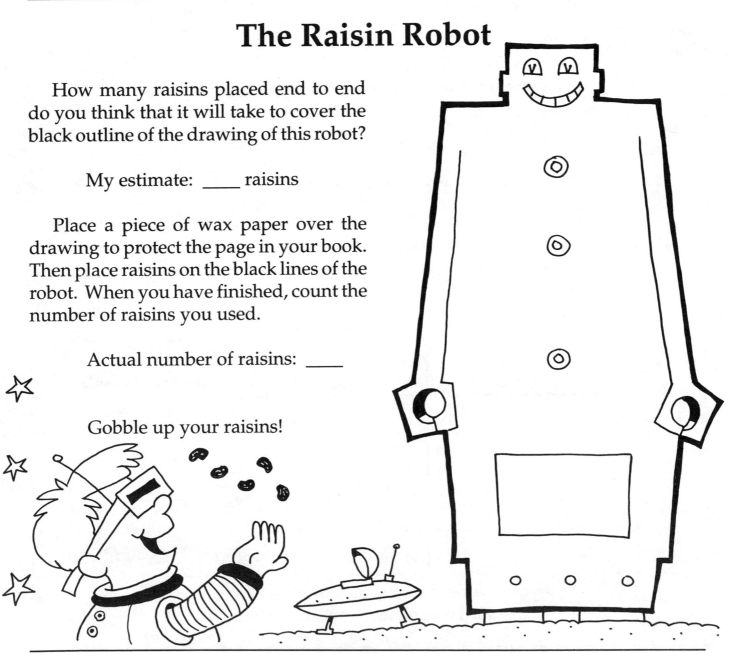

How many raisins placed end to end do you think that it will take to cover the black outline of the drawing of this robot?

My estimate: ____ raisins

Place a piece of wax paper over the drawing to protect the page in your book. Then place raisins on the black lines of the robot. When you have finished, count the number of raisins you used.

Actual number of raisins: ____

Gobble up your raisins!

Serving Sizes

How many peas do you estimate it will take to fill one-half cup? First, make an estimate. Now count the peas. How close did you come?

Fill a one-half measuring cup with each of the foods below. You can fill four different cups, or empty your cup and start over with each new food. Have fun estimating and then counting the food items. Color in the drawing of each food for which your estimate is no more than 10 pieces over or under the actual count.

food item	my estimate	actual count	My estimate was within 10 of the actual count.
frozen peas			
grapes			
raisins			
cereal			

If you colored in three or four of the pictures,
consider yourself an incredible estimator!

How Much is "a Cup"?

Use a pitcher, drinking glass, and bowl to practice estimating. First, fill a one-cup measuring cup with juice. Then put a piece of masking tape on an empty pitcher to mark how high you estimate one cup of juice will come when it is poured into the container. Do the same with the glass and the bowl.

Next, pour the juice into the pitcher. Does the juice come higher or lower than the masking tape? Or was your estimate right on the mark? _____

Now pour the juice into the glass. Is it above, below, or right at the masking tape? _____

Finally, pour the juice into the bowl. Is it above, below, or right at the tape? _____

Was your estimate most accurate for the pitcher, the glass, or the bowl? _____

Color the drawing of that container. Enjoy your juice!

Fruit Freeze

How much fruit juice do you estimate that it will take to fill an ice cube tray?

I think it will take (make a check mark by your estimate):

- ❑ 1/4 cup
- ❑ 1/2 cup
- ❑ 3/4 cup
- ❑ 1 cup
- ❑ 1 1/2 cups
- ❑ 2 cups
- ❑ 2 1/2 cups
- ❑ 3 cups
- ❑ other _____

Fill an empty ice cube tray with fruit juice. Then pour the juice into a one-quart measuring cup to see how close your estimate came. You then have two yummy choices. You can pour the juice into a glass and drink it. Or, pour the juice back into the ice cube tray. Put the tray into the freezer. Enjoy gobbling up frozen fruit treats when the cubes are frozen.

Tablespoon Tease

How many tablespoons of milk are in one-third cup of milk? Record your estimate and then check your answers by using a tablespoon to measure the milk. Repeat for one-fourth cup and one-half cup of milk.

one-third cup:
    estimate: _____ tablespoons
    actual measurement: _____ tablespoons

one-fourth cup:
    estimate: _____ tablespoons
    actual measurement: _____ tablespoons

one-half cup:
    estimate: _____ tablespoons
    actual measurement: _____ tablespoons

Which of your estimates was the most accurate? _____
Color in the drawing of that measuring cup.

Did measuring one-fourth cup of milk help you accurately estimate how many tablespoons of milk are in one-half cup? _____

Sunflower Seed Sensation

Fill a one-fourth measuring cup with sunflower seeds. Count the seeds. One-fourth cup = _____ sunflower seeds.
Using the information above, estimate and then count the number of sunflower seeds it will take to completely fill:

one-half cup
my estimate _____
actual number _____

one cup
my estimate _____
actual number _____

Edible Estimates Certificate

This certifies that

_____

has successfully completed the Edible Estimates
section of
Gobble Up Math.

Signature of Chef _____

Date _____

Bibliography for Children

"Gobble up" these books with children. Enjoy exploring math and nutrition concepts through books while experiencing hands-on math and nutrition activities in *Gobble Up Math*.

The Amazing Book of Shapes, Lydia Sharman, Dorling Kindersley Publishing, Inc., 1994.

Anno's Hat Tricks, Akihiro Nozaki and Mitsumasa Anno, Philomel Books, 1985.

Anno's Math Games, Mitsumasa Anno, Philomel Books, 1991.

Anno's Mysterious Multiplying Jar, Mitsumasa Anno, Philomel Books, 1993.

Each Orange Had Eight Slices, Paul Giganti, Jr., Greenwillow Books, 1992.

Eating Fractions, Bruce MacMillan, Scholastic, 1991.

Help Is On the Way for Math Skills, Marilyn Berry, Children's Press, 1985.

How Many Snails? Paul Giganti, Jr., Greenwillow Books, 1988.

How Much Is a Million? David M. Schwartz, Lothrop, Lee, and Shepard Books, 1985.

Janice VanCleave's Math for Every Kid, Janice VanCleave, Wiley, 1991.

Knowabout Capacity, Henry Arthur Pluckrose, Franklin Watts, 1988.

Knowabout Sorting, Henry Arthur Pluckrose, Franklin Watts, 1988.

Math-a-Magic, Laurence B. White, Whitman, 1990.

Math for Smarty Pants, Marilyn Burns, Little, Brown and Company, 1982.

Mathematics, Irving Adler, Doubleday, 1990.

Multiplying and Dividing, Annabel Thomas, Highgate Press, 1985.

Number Art, Leonard Everett Ficher, Four Winds Press, 1982.

One, Two, Buckle My Shoe, Sam Brown, Gryphon House, 1982.

Socrates and the Three Little Pigs, Mitsumasa Anno, Philomel Books, 1985.

Weighing and Measuring, Annabel Thomas, Highgate Press, 1986.

The World of Numbers, Paul Berman, Marshall Cavendish Corporation, 1989.